Unbelievable Designing Ideas for Bathroom

Get Innovative with Eco-friendly Bathroom designs

Janek Arango

DISCLAIMER

This information is provided and sold with the knowledge that the publisher and author do not offer any legal or other professional advice. In the case of a need for any such expertise consult with the appropriate professional. This book does not contain all information available on the subject. This book has not been created to be specific to any individual's or organizations' situation or needs. Every effort has been made to make this book as accurate as possible. However, there may be typographical and or content errors. Therefore, this book should serve only as a general guide and not as the ultimate source of subject information. This book contains information that might be dated and is intended only to educate and entertain. The author and publisher shall have no liability or responsibility to any person or entity regarding any loss or damage incurred, or alleged to have incurred, directly or indirectly, by the information contained in this book.

Thank you for downloading this book. Please review on Amazon for us so that I can make future versions even better. A portion of the proceeds from this book goes to American Cancer Society®. Thank you for you support. God bless.

Just for Downloading this book and showing your support, I wanna give you 2 of our other books, absolutely **FREE**. Just go to the link and subscribe and get **2 Free Books** for your support. Don't forget to give us **5 star Rating** so we can make better versions to help more people. Thank you guys for your support.

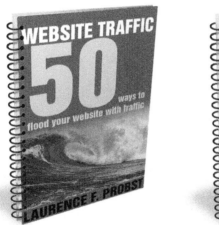 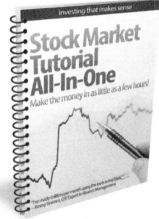

Click Here to Download-Free Website Traffic & How To Invest in The Stock Market

Table of Contents

Foreword

A lot of people want to live in an eco friendly house; you probably are one of them too right? Why? Well, this simple consideration is enough to help the earth because they want to embark recycling efforts for a much essential cause of being able to live in great harmony with the environment – eco living. Get all the info you need here.

Chapter 1

Introduction

Synopsis

Eco living is all about living your life, as a person and as community, such that it's sustainable and ideal for earth. In essence, living a greener life involves these principles:

- Conserve energy
- Conserve resources
- Reduce waste
- Reduce pollution as well as emission of hazardous substances to the environment
- Protect the ecological balance of the earth along with the other living beings.

Why Living Eco Green Is Essential?

Well, as more and more nations are becoming affluent and developed, as more and more communities are embracing a culture of 'consumerism', and lots of industries take action to meet the demands for various services and goods though the process of mass production, it generally becomes inevitable that energy and resources are being utilized and used at tremendously rapid rates.

In addition to that, pollutants as well as harmful substances are being released to the environment, more and more materials are being discarded as nothing but wastes at extremely unsustainable rates. Because of this, because of the activities such as deforestation or mining in order to extract various resources from earth, and because of the pollution created from these processes, people have upset the earth's ecological balance affecting the many plants and living creatures on earth.

The way that human race are living nowadays is definitely not sustainable. At the current rate that people are using the energy and different resources of the earth, they would possibly run out soon and worst, nothing would be left. And as people wiped away plant and animal species through irresponsible activities, soon there will be nothing left.

Some people would argue and claim that there's a cost in living green.

However, this is only a small cost compared to the costs that people will pay if nothing will be changed in order to protect and save the environment.

Eco Friendly Homes

There are lots of things for you to do in order to live in an eco friendly home and have a greener lifestyle.

Aside from adopting the 'Reduce Reuse Recycle' principle, you can actually adopt various energy-saving practices. There are actually lots of energy efficient appliances and practices for you to adopt in order to make your home an energy efficient, green home.

Why don't you help by reducing the pollution? Reduce the use of hazardous substances and chemical, and use eco-friendly home cleaners as well as other environment-friendly products for your everyday needs.

Help introduce more trees and plant in your environment and motivate others to make action as well. Grow a green garden with the use of green gardening practices. There are lots of things that you can consider to help build a greener environment – start from living green and living in an eco friendly home.

Chapter 2

Benefits Of Eco-Friendly Homes

Synopsis

More and more homeowners are becoming aware and conscious about protecting the environment and are opting to a green building principle. Because of this, designers, architects, and builders are incorporating green materials and elements in homes that are being built. With the developments and advancements in technology, and because of the emergence of various building concepts, homeowners can integrate green elements without the need to sacrifice the entire appeal and appearance of their homes.

Despite the increased interest by numerous sectors about green building concepts, lots of homeowners still don't know and understand what constitutes green homes and how these eco friendly homes are being built. An eco friendly home has lots of beneficial effects and results on the overall health and well being of families and it's also a very financially sound idea.

Benefits

Healthy Home

An eco friendly home utilizes toxin free building materials, ensuring that people inside the house are generally free from all harmful pollutants and elements that are usually present in a traditional home.

Cost Efficient Home

The cost of maintaining an eco friendly home is the same or even lesser than the maintenance cost of a traditional and standard home. Yes, the initial cost is possibly high, but the future savings that you'll be able to generate later is sufficient enough for you to offset the initial investment. You will certainly save about 40 percent from your monthly electricity bill and 50 percent from water consumption. In addition to that, eco friendly homes are much more durable as compared to standard homes. This translates and equates to lesser maintenance and repair. Moreover, a green home value much higher compared to a standard home this is the reason why the demands for eco friendly homes are steadily increasing.

Environment Friendly Home

The heating and cooling of homes usually account to more or less 20 percent of the total used energy from a typical or standard household. Add to this the standard energy requirements from all the household appliances, lighting and other electronic equipments and you'll see why standard homes are being considered as a segment that uses and consumes lots of energy. On the contrary, eco friendly home consume less 40 percent of energy.

Nowadays, there are eco friendly homes that have the capacity of reducing their dependence from conventional energy sources, and they have this added capability of generating their very own energy with the use of alternative energy sources like geothermal, biomass, wind, and sun.

Eco friendly homes have highly efficient plumbing and bathing fixtures. They adopt landscaping designs that are drought tolerant. Eco friendly homes can also make use of excellent irrigation systems equipped with beneficial water conserving features. These combined features and elements can cut water consumption for almost 50%.

Increased Security And Safety

Eco friendly homes have much higher security and safety standards as compared to regular homes. They are basically equipped with excellent and high performing smoke detectors, gadgets that detect radon and carbon dioxide emissions, security systems, and techniques of delivering termite treatments and pesticide.

Lesser natural resources are being used in building an eco friendly home. This alone can be considered as an excellent boost in campaigns of saving the natural resources. A huge portion of materials used to build a green home are basically recycled materials.

So what do you think? Isn't it a great option to have an eco friendly home?

Chapter 3

Features Of Eco-Friendly Homes

Synopsis

With more people preferring to live in an eco friendly home that is in harmony with the environment, more builders and architects are offering environment friendly designs to address the ever growing demands for green homes. The negative effects on earth are becoming more and more visible nowadays. People are now more aware about the damages that irresponsible human activities have brought, however, it is inevitable. But there are lots of ways and methods that you can use to help introduce a green environment. And one of these is to live in an eco friendly home.

Eco Friendly Home Features

If you are after saving the environment, you should aim to decrease carbon emission. However, most homes aren't eco friendly enough that it can lessen this count. In fact, majority of homes are emitting gases over the normal amount. If this continues, the world will become a big sauna. As a result, glaciers will melt rising the level of water. Rising level of water can actually lead to land mass disappearing. And when rain pours hard, it can cause flooding. Flooding then will cause illnesses and death. It is really a domino effect; moreover, this is only a factor of what will happen if gases keep on rising. To have an eco friendly home equipped with environment friendly features allow you to help contain gas emission to a minimum.

- Your eco friendly property doesn't have to be excessively big or small. It needs to be large enough to let everybody have their own space. It needs to be adequate enough for it to be maintained cost effectively and efficiently.

- Consider its location. An eco friendly home is usually situated in excellent locations. It is usually a part of one green community with homes that have eco friendly features. The surrounding is usually filled with environment friendly landscaping regardless if it's a business establishment or a residential home.

- An eco friendly home is one that is equipped with energy efficient appliances. Meaning anything that is installed inside the property consumes lesser energy as compared to old appliances. And because of this, you will be able to enjoy huge savings from utilities expenses.

- Eco friendly homes are generally made from sustainable materials. The materials used to build an eco friendly home are highly abundant locally; they also come from all renewable resources – materials that are organic such as wood, plants, or animals. Of course, some of the materials used are synthetic but they are used minimally.

- Eco friendly homes are equipped with passive solar system, meaning they are being oriented to utilize and maximize benefits from using natural sunlight.

- Eco homes are well insulated. Their walls have an inert gas layer that functions to keep the air warm during winter seasons and design to maintain cool unruffled air during the summer seasons.

- Most eco friendly homes are automated, allowing homeowners to manage and monitor essential features such as smoke detection, security, even energy consumption.

- In building eco homes, paints that aren't volatile are being used posing no risks to the health of the occupants.

Chapter 4

Considerations For Buying An Eco-Friendly Home

Synopsis

With lots of options to choose from and factors to consider in buying a home, it is likely one of the most complicated buying decision that you can ever make. And purchasing an eco friendly home requires much more consideration.

It is never easy to choose a home that can satisfy every unique need, thus try to choose one that can accommodate most of your unique needs and requirements.

In buying an eco friendly and being an eco conscious customer, aside from making a rational choice, you will want that your purchase reflects your many environmental convictions.

Factors to consider as you start your quest may include all the green features that are most essential to you, great locations for an eco friendly home, financing of green home, and choosing an agent or realtor who basically knows all about 'green' real estate market.

Buying Vs. Building

Different homes are eco friendly in different factors, but all of them are equipped with one common thing – efficiency. Well, the efficiency of the home is the actually the key. Energy efficient features of an eco home are not just a green choice but it also helps you save money. Yes, new homes may be considered more eco friendly as compared to older homes because they can be outfitted with energy efficient appliances, low VOC paints, as well as low flow shower heads. In addition to that, building a new home rather than purchasing one may mean that you have the option to choose what eco friendly features you want.

Eco Renovation

If you are not into building a new eco friendly home, buying one that is not eco friendly and having some major renovations to make it an eco home is also an option. However, either option can be pricey.

Even though you're going to realize major cost savings in the future, you will pay more money for buying or building a green eco friendly home instead of standard one. Purchasing an existing house – especially one foreclosure property – will cost you less initially, but you must also consider the potential burdensome factors and cost of your eco friendly renovation.

Non Eco Priorities

There are also other priorities that you should take into careful consideration- is living in a great school district essential to you? How about the proximity to facilities, work, recreation, and restaurants? How about your budget? If you want to live in an eco friendly home, but you have to live close downtown and if you have concerns regarding your limited budget, then your plan may need to be postponed and deferred until your retirement. Do some research, plan carefully, and consider all the necessary factors.

Consider Relocation

If an eco friendly home is what you are after, then you may need to consider relocating to another place of region. So, if you research appears fruitless, consider focusing your sights to a place that has lots to offer.

Looking For A Green Real Estate Agent

It is always best to look for a reliable realtor who can help and assist you in finding that perfect home for you and your family. It is even better if this person also specialized in an eco friendly listing.

Chapter 5

Building Your Own Eco-Friendly Home

Synopsis

Eco friendly homes are built using processes that are resource efficient and environmentally responsible. All facets of the home from interior to exterior design are provided with eco friendly features. Even construction, maintenance, and operation are performed in ways that don't affect and endanger the environment.

Building

- Site Conditions: Before planning in building your new home, you should consider the best site. Choose an area that suits your wants and needs. It should be able to offer space for various solar accesses, water, air, privacy, gardens.

- Building materials: If you really are after building an eco friendly home, you should use environmental friendly materials. You can use ceramics, cement, aluminum, bricks, steel, and glass as the raw materials. Before, wood is considered as a primary material in eco friendly homes but because of the illegal logging issue, it was replaced with aluminum and mild steel. In addition to that, you should also use non toxic paint, LED lightings, recycled tiles, recycled glass, recycled aluminum, as well as other recycled products and materials.

- Rooms: Consider room locations and the amount of natural air and sunlight that can enter through it. Also consider the amount of natural heat to enter the rooms in certain time of day.

- Home Layout: Most eco friendly homes are equipped with open design layout to reduce the cost of construction. It also enhances ventilation and light. It is also easier to manage and arrange the furniture with open spaces.

- Roofing: Green roofing – its attractive and very cost efficient. With green roofing, you will be able to have extra insulation keeping your energy consumption low.

- Wall Materials: Use materials that have the ability of absorbing solar heat such as fabricated or natural brick. Bricks that are made from cement, lime, sand, etc. are great because they are resistant to fire, they absorb heat from the sun, and they have lower water absorption.

- Flooring Materials: Depending upon the function of the room, you can actually choose from varieties of flooring options and materials such as parquet, marble, terrazzo, granite, wood, bamboo, and ceramic. But when it comes to an eco friendly flooring, bamboo and laminated wood can be the best option especially when it comes to the bedroom.

- Utilize Solar Panels: Solar panels are becoming more and more popular to eco friendly consumers. These are being used as an alternative source for electrical energy. Aside from its economic benefits, it can give you protection from short circuits and fires.

Having an eco friendly home is a simple step that can help save the environment in some ways and it also offers potentially vital benefits to homeowners. This is a simple yet excellent way of exerting an effort that aims toward the improvement of the earth – a role for the nature. Thus, instead of designing your home for your benefit, why not consider building it instead? Try to consider the amount of resources and energy that you can save from building it. This is already helping the environment. And it also helps you in giving your family a healthy, assured, and safe future.

Chapter 6

Designing Tips for Eco-Friendly Home

Synopsis

Having an eco-friendly home provides countless benefits. It helps in reducing negative impacts on the environment and allows you to understand how to live with the use of green home decorations. If you have an eco-friendly home, it is easy for you to create a tempting ambiance.

Creating an eco-friendly home is not a daunting task. If you want to change your home style into a green space, you need to expand your ideas. How can you do this? To get enough ideas on how to design your house, simply take this article as your guide.

Effective Tips to Have an Eco-friendly Home

To have an eco-friendly home, you don't need to spend more time and effort. Since it is all about minimizing your available resources, you will never spend huge money. For your guide, here are the top green home design tips you shouldn't miss to know:

- Get Local for Home Furnishings - If you want to get a green home décor, don't forget to have an eco-friendly fixture and furniture. Before buying, make sure that you know where to deal with. Not all shops are offering the best and genuine quality. So, don't forget to conduct a research before purchasing.

- Get Live Houseplants - To add green style to your space, you shouldn't miss to get lice houseplants. The typical examples of these are snake plant, spider plant, philodendron, pothos and a lot more.

- Get Indoor Paint - This indoor paint can combat the toxic in the space. To have this, you need to choose organic finishes and paints that are free of toxins. As an option, you can get the Bioshield and Ecos.

- Use Eco-friendly Flooring – To have a green home style, you can have the best flooring type in the market. The common examples of these are bamboo, linoleum, reclaimed wood and cork. These eco-friendly flooring can help in changing your home design and appearance.
- Using Lights with Timers - Though you need to light up your home, you should know how to conserve energy. You can do this with the use of timer lights. You can get these lights with timers in various shops.
- Foster Your Outdoor Living Space - You can do this through improving your backyard's style and appearance. Depending on your choice, you are free to add attractive birdhouses, feeders and other outdoor decorations.

Aside from the above mentioned, you can also have a green home style through adding heat and air condition using renewable energy. One of the most common green home designs is the solar panel installation. It helps in reducing energy consumption and makes energy for use. Depending on your choice, you can also use natural gas for heating and air conditioning.

Eco-friendly Home – Why Do You Need to Have One?

At present days, more and more people are longing to have an eco-friendly home. If you don't know the benefits of having a green home style, here they are:

- Helps in Reducing Water and Energy Bills – The construction of a green home starts with its simple designs. Before improving your home style, you need to know the available resources that suit for your preferred designs. As a result, you have a chance to save more monthly expenses.

- Enhanced Indoor Air Quality – Every material used in the green home construction is environmentally friendly. The typical examples of these are harvested plantation lumber, recycled timber, hemp and straw. These materials can help in emitting harmful gases and thus improve indoor air quality.

- Higher Resale Value – If you have a certified green home, you can get a higher resale value. This is essential, particularly when you are planning to sell your house.

- Increased Security and Safety – Eco-friendly home has security and safe standards compared to regular homes. This space is loaded with quality gadgets to detect radon emissions and carbon monoxide. It is also filled with fool proof security systems to remove termites and pesticides.

Other benefits of having a green home style are financing incentives, promoting the use of eco-friendly products and greater comfort for your family members.

Chapter 7

Furnish Your Home with Eco-Friendly Furniture

Synopsis

Whether you are living in an apartment, dorm or in your own house, you need furniture to offer a place to eat, sit, sleep and store your valuable stuff. To have some furniture units, you will consider various things to get your preferred style.

If you want an eco-friendly home, you shouldn't miss to know the different green furniture units. With these green products, you can improve your health, budget and save Mother Earth.

However, choosing the best green furniture units requires enough time. Since there are various selections to choose from, you need to conduct an extensive research to have the best one.

Tips on How to Choose Eco-friendly Home Furniture

Eco-friendly furniture can really change your space. Depending on your choice, you can pick the simple or stylish type. For your guide, here are some tips you need to consider in buying green furniture items:

- Purchase Bamboo Furniture, Flooring and Window Blind Products - The material used in these items doesn't contain any harmful elements. Therefore, they will never cause a little damage to the environment.
- Get Quality and Durable Furniture - Through getting these units, you are certain that they will last for several years. It means that you don't need to change your furniture every year.

You will also use their ultimate purpose without spending more cash.

- Purchase Wood Products - Your preferred wood products must be certified by the Forest Stewardship Council or

FCS. This is your indicator that your preferred units are come from forestry operations.

- Get Furniture with Recycled Materials – You can easily find these units in various shops. The typical examples of these are wood from mold homes, resurrected items found at the bottom of lakes and a lot more.
- Shop at Antique, Vintage and Consignment Shops – Most of these shops offer cheap but quality eco-friendly furniture.

Depending on your choice, you can purchase via online or local store.

Getting the different types of green furniture can be easily done. Like other homeowners, you can get the recycled furniture. This unit is often built from older pieces. Some of them are made of wood while others are metal.

If you want more options, you can also get furniture items with natural materials. These units are not made from recycled materials. Instead, they come from renewable resources. The common materials used in these units are bamboo, wood and hemp.

Chapter 8

The Eco-Friendly Bathroom Ideas

Synopsis

Do you want to have an eco-friendly home? Then, you need to change your space style into a green home design. Aside from your interior and kitchen space, you also need to improve the appearance of your bathroom.

To create an eco-friendly bathroom, you need consider various things.

If you don't know how to do it, simple take the succeeding guides:

Some Ideas

Step 1: Buy Ceramic Tiles – You can use these tiles for countertops, floors and walls surrounding the shower and tub. These ceramic tiles are susceptible from moisture. Some of them are made from recycled products while others are not. Aside from these tiles, you can also use finished bamboo and linoleum for the best flooring styles.

Step 2: Install a Low-Flow Shower Head – This is your best option to have a green bathroom design. With low-flow shower head, you can save money on energy and water bills. The typical shower heads use has 6 gallons per minute.

Step 3: Install an Ultra-Low Flush Toilet - This can also help in saving more water. Dual-flush toilets have two knobs. This style allows users to conserved water through selecting the amount needed for flushing waste.

Step 4: Look for Wheatboard Cabinets - These cabinets are often made from non-toxic binder and wheat straw. Cabinets made from MDF can emit toxic chemicals like formaldehyde. With these materials, they are proven safe to use and eco-friendly.

Step 5: Install a Bath Fan – This can help in reducing moisture and mold. Just make sure that the fan is safe for installation over showers and tubs. Whatever types of bath fan you want, you can get it in various shops.

Top Eco-friendly Bathroom Ideas

Renovating your bathroom can change your space style. You can do this through adding fixtures and other stuff. For your guide, here are the top eco-friendly and effective bathroom ideas you shouldn't miss to consider:

- Natural Organic Materials - You can go green through the use of natural flooring, linens and cabinetry. To make your bathroom more stylish than before, use curve and oval shapes. You can also use recycled and modern finishes.
- Spa Central – Whirlpool tubs and soaker can help in designing your bathroom. You can also add heated towel bars mounted beside the tub. This can offer the most comfortable exit from a bubbly and hot bath.
- Faucets and Fixtures – In getting these items, you have to look for modern and stunning styles. For best option, you

can add lavatory faucets, showerheads, toilets and a lot more.

Through considering these eco-friendly ideas, you can easily change your bathroom styles. If you don't know what to pick from, simply ask assistance from experts.

Chapter 9

Eco-friendly Household Products in the Market

Synopsis

To go green, you need to purchase eco-friendly household products. However, not all homeowners are aware with these multiple items. If you are one of them, you are on the right spot.

Going green doesn't require more cash. You just need to know the different eco-friendly products that suit for your needs and styles. To expand your ideas about the different green products in the market, here are some of them:

Products

- Infrared Thermometer - This is a handy and cheap little gadget. It can help you in reducing you energy bills. This household item can be found in various shops, both local and online stores. You just need to pick the best shop to get the genuine type.
- Programmable Thermostat - This is one of the best and intelligent devices. It gives you control over your space's temperature and energy use. It also allows you to view and adjust your thermostat remotely.
- LED Light Bulbs - These bulbs can help you in saving more energy and money. Whatever brands you have, make sure that you are familiar with its features and styles. You also need to check its exact price for great savings.

Apart from the above mentioned, you can also get the different homemade products. Similar with other homeowners, you can have the un-paper towels, reusable swiffer dusters, solid shampoo bars, reusable sandwich bags and a lot more.

To get these eco-friendly household products, you need to consider various things. At first, you need to check its warning labels. Some manufacturers don't list the different ingredients of their products.

Therefore, you have to watch for their labels. You need to check the warning signs like "vapors harmful", "caution" and a lot more. In addition, it is also best to depend on honest advertising and minimal packaging.

Chapter 10

Using Alternative Energy for Eco-Friendly Home

Synopsis

To go green, various people are using alternative energy at home. If you don't know the different types of green energy, you need to read this chapter as your guide.

Green Energy Types – What are They?:

Energy

Alternative energy comes in various types. Here are they:

- Hydropower – This type of energy converts water from rivers into valuable energy released from turbines. Before, it was used for operation of machinery and irrigation.

As time passes by, people use hydropower to build hydropower plants to create mass amounts of electricity.

- Geothermal - This is produced from hot or steam water from the surface of the Earth. The vapor powers electric generators through rotating turbines. Geothermal is use for heating buildings.

- Wind - This is often used to create energy by rotating huge propeller like blades. These blades slow down the speed of the wind and channel it to the generator that generates electricity.

- Solar – This is use to power some homes, agriculture and cars. This energy type is usually huge and occupies more space.

- Hydrogen – This is also one of the eco-friendly energy you shouldn't miss to know. It can help in producing unlimited amount of energy with the use of electricity and water.

After knowing these alternative energy types, you will be tempted to use them. The main question is, how can you use these types to save more cash?

Effective Green Alternative Energy Tips

To save more energy using this alternative solution, the first thing that you need to do is to start switching to green power. You can do this through catching the attention of your current provider. Then, start plug-in to solar power. You also need to get passive solar to work for you.

Like other homeowners, you can use solar power to heat the water for your dishwasher, shower and laundry. In addition, you can also heat your home with the use of biofuel. For additional guide, you can take the following tips as your guide:

1. Reduce Phantom Loads - This refers to the energy that an appliance consumes when it is turned off. You can do this through unplugging appliances and other electronic systems, especially when not in use.

2. Use Energy-Efficient Appliances – You can find these appliances in various shops. You just need to check the energy star appliance between 10-20% ales energy.

3. Install a Thermostat – This can automatically adjust the temperature of your home. In case you forgot to adjust your thermostat, a programmable type could save you as high as 15% on cooling and heating costs.

4. Install Efficient Windows – Window glass is a slender barrier against outside temperatures. If you don't know what to pick from, you can ask assistance from experts. Depending on your preferred installer, you need to spend enough cash. But, its rewards are very remarkable.

5. Conserve Water - This can help in lowering your energy and water bill. As advised, you can take faster shower. You also need to be more conscious while washing dishes or clothes. If not in use, don't forget to turn off the faucet.

As you have noticed, there are several ways on how to conserve energy. You just need to know on how to use the alternative solutions. With your knowledge about eco-friendly products and solutions, you don't need to worry about your budget. You can easily change the appearance and style of your house.

Whether you have a small or huge house, you have to go green. Eco-friendly home brings safe and healthy environment.

This is the main reason why most people prefer to use green products and solutions.

Can't wait to go green? Then, the choice is yours! With green home, you and your family are totally secured. Therefore, you are certain that they are free from any harmful elements. At the same time, you can save more cash. So, don't miss this chance and learn how to go green. Understand why most people love eco-friendly products and home styles and be amazed!

CPSIA information can be obtained at www.ICGtesting.com
Printed in the USA
LVOW03s2307060115

421813LV00005B/69/P